Roses Among Thorns

Other books by St. Francis de Sales
from Sophia Institute Press:

Thy Will Be Done!

Finding God's Will for You

The Art of Loving God

The Sign of the Cross

St. Francis de Sales

Roses Among Thorns

Simple Advice for Renewing
Your Spiritual Journey

Edited and translated
by Christopher O. Blum

SOPHIA INSTITUTE PRESS
Manchester, New Hampshire

This volume contains an original selection of passages from the letters of St. Francis de Sales, newly translated from volumes 12 through 15 of the Annecy edition of his *Oeuvres complètes* (J. Nierat and E. Vitte, publishers, 1902-1908).

Except where otherwise noted, biblical references in this book are taken from the Catholic Edition of the Revised Standard Version of the Bible, copyright 1965, 1966 by the Division of Christian Education of the National Council of the Churches of Christ in the United States of America. Used by permission. All rights reserved.

Sophia Institute Press
Box 5284, Manchester, NH 03108
1-800-888-9344

www.SophiaInstitute.com

Sophia Institute Press® is a registered trademark of Sophia Institute.

Library of Congress Cataloging-in-Publication Data
Francis, de Sales, Saint, 1567-1622.
   [Works. Selections. English. 2014]
   Roses among thorns : simple advice for renewing your spiritual journey /
St. Francis de Sales ; edited and translated by Christopher O. Blum.
      pages cm
   "This volume contains an original selection of passages from the letters
of St. Francis de Sales, newly translated from volumes 12 through 15 of the
Annecy edition of his Oeuvres completes (J. Nierat and E. Vitte, publishers,
1902-1908)."—E-Cip t.p. verso.
   ISBN 978-1-62282-206-5 (pbk. : alk. paper) 1. Spiritual life—Catholic
Church. I. Blum, Christopher Olaf, 1969- translator. II. Title.
   BX2350.3.F72 2014
   248.4'82--dc23

                                                                    2014006111

First printing

❧

Contents

❧

Foreword

I have had a longtime admiration for St. Francis de Sales.

I became a Catholic in 1975, and shortly after my conversion, I was given a copy of St. Francis de Sales's *Introduction to the Devout Life*. The wisdom of this saint formed my spirituality and my early practice of the Faith. I still return to St. Francis de Sales and recommend his writings regularly to those beginning the path of discipleship.

In 2008, thirty-three years after I became a Catholic, I was ordained a bishop, and I chose a phrase from St. Francis de Sales—*Cor ad cor loquitor* ("Heart speaks to heart")—for my episcopal motto.

I was not the first to choose that motto. In fact, I chose it because my spiritual mentor, Blessed John Henry Cardinal Newman, chose it upon being appointed a cardinal. What he saw, and what I saw, in the words of St. Francis de Sales was an understanding that grace works through ordinary men and women—disciples of Jesus Christ—who reflect the truth, beauty, and goodness of Jesus Christ.

In some ways, the work of St. Francis de Sales precedes the Second Vatican Council's call to the universal vocation of holiness. At the beginning of *Introduction to the Devout Life*, de Sales remarks that "it is an error, or rather a heresy, to say devotion is incompatible with the life of a soldier, a tradesman, a prince, or a married woman.... It has happened that many have lost perfection in the desert who had preserved it in the world."

Today, more than ever, Catholic men and women need clear instruction in the path of Christian discipleship. We have, unfortunately, lost many of the great practices of piety and devotion that form Catholic culture and Catholic conscience. There is beauty in mortification, in order, and in piety; and the work of St. Francis captures that beauty.

St. Francis de Sales gives direction in prayer, devotion, discernment, and mortification, in a way that can be understood and implemented in the midst of ordinary life. He understands clearly the movements of the soul, the affections and temptations that draw us from Jesus Christ. He also understands the antidote. His work is a guidebook for anyone who seeks a deeper relationship with Jesus Christ.

Foreword

Roses Among Thorns offers newly translated meditations from the works of St. Francis de Sales that Catholic men and women — lay, clerical, or religious — can reflect on prayerfully. This book can be used as a devotional or in spiritual direction or in the sacrament of penance.

St. Francis de Sales understood that Christ is revealed as one heart speaks to another. I pray that the heart of the great saint, reflected in these meditations, will reflect to you the Sacred Heart of Jesus Christ.

— Most Rev. James D. Conley,
Bishop of Lincoln,
February 27, 2014

Roses Among Thorns

1

❦

Seasons of Life

All of the seasons of life come together in the soul. Sometimes we feel winter's sterility, distraction, distaste, and boredom, sometimes spring's dew, with the fragrance of holy blossoms, and sometimes a burning desire to please our good God. What remains is autumn, and even then we may see no great harvest.

Yet it often happens that in threshing the wheat and pressing the grape we find a greater yield than we had expected. We want it always to be spring and summer, but there must be vicissitudes of the interior life as well as the exterior.

Only in heaven will everything be springtime in its beauty, autumn in its fruitfulness, and summer in its ardor. There will be no winter there; but here winter is necessary for the work of abnegation and for the thousand minor but beautiful virtues that we exercise in a fallow time.

Let us, then, continue to put one foot in front of the other. Provided our hearts be true, we will walk aright.

2

❦

Jesus the Gardener

Do not be anxious. Rouse yourself to serve the Lord with steadfastness, attentiveness, and meekness. That is the true way to serve him. If you can refrain from trying to do all things, but instead attempt to do only some one thing, then you will do much. Practice the mortifications that most often present themselves to you, for that is the first duty to be done. After that you can take up the others. Lovingly kiss the crosses that our Lord himself lays upon your arms, without looking to see whether they are of precious or aromatic wood. They are more truly crosses when they are made of a wood that smells dirty and is considered useless.

Mary Magdalene tried to hold on to our Lord; she wanted him for herself. His appearance was not as she had wished it to be, which is why she looked at him without recognizing him. She wanted to see him arrayed in glory, not in the common clothes of a gardener. Yet in the end she knew that it was he when he said to her, "Mary" (John 20:14-16). You see, it is our Lord garbed as a gardener whom we meet day by day, here and there, in the ordinary mortifications that present themselves to us. We want more noble-seeming ones. But the ones that seem the most noble are not the best. Before we see him in his glory, he wants to plant many humble flowers in our garden, according to his plan. This is why he is dressed the way he is. Our task is to let our hearts be ever united to his, and our wills to his pleasure.

3

Roses Among Thorns

Let us make our way through the low valleys of the humble little virtues. There we will see roses among thorns: charity shining forth amid interior and exterior affliction, lilies of purity, and violets of mortification. We ought to love above all others these three small virtues: meekness of heart, poverty of spirit, and simplicity of life, together with those common labors of visiting the sick, serving the poor, and consoling the afflicted. Yet let it all be done freely and without anxiety. No, our arms are not strong enough for us to climb the cedars of Lebanon; let us be content with the hyssop that grows in the valleys.

4

Choosing Virtue

Be very meek. You should live not according to your passions and your inclinations, but according to reason and devotion. Love tenderly those who have been given to you by the hand of our Lord. Be very humble toward all. Direct your mind toward peace and tranquillity, and suffocate your bad inclinations by attending diligently to the practice of the contrary virtues. Mark well these words: you are suffering because you fear vice more than you love virtue. If you were able to stir your heart a little more deeply to the practice of meekness and true humility, you would be courageous. But you must frequently think of it. Prepare yourself to do so first thing each morning, and God will send you a thousand consolations. And do not forget to lift your heart to God and your thoughts to eternity.

5

❦

A Pattern of Devotion

Here in short compass are the exercises that I recommend. First, when you arise, briefly prepare yourself for the whole day. Then your mental prayer should be before the noon meal, when you are otherwise unoccupied, and for about an hour at a time. Retreat briefly in the evening before supper, and, by way of repetition, make a dozen lively aspirations to God, in accord with your morning's meditation or on some other subject.

During the day and between its tasks, as often as you can, you should examine yourself to see whether your affections have been distracted by some object, and whether you are still holding our Lord by the hand. Should you find yourself at a loss, gather your soul together and set it at rest. Imagine yourself like our Lady, calmly working with one hand while holding on to our Lord with the other, or holding him with her other arm during his infancy.

In times of peace and tranquillity, multiply your acts of humility, for by this means you will accustom your heart to meekness. Do not attempt to combat by argument the little temptations that arise; instead, simply bring your heart back to Jesus Christ crucified.

Do not trouble yourself to make many vocal prayers, and always, when you pray and you sense your heart carried to mental prayer, let it go there straightaway, and should your mental prayer be accompanied by only the Lord's Prayer, the Angelic Salutation, and the Creed, you may be content.

6

Jesus in Our Heart

How happy you will be if while you are in the world you keep Jesus Christ in your heart! Remember the principal lesson he left to us, and in only a few short words, so that we would be able to remember it: "Learn of me, for I am meek, and humble of heart" (Matt. 11:29, Douay-Rheims). It is everything to have a heart that is meek toward our neighbor and humble toward God. At every moment give such a heart to our Savior, and let it be the heart of your heart. You will see that to the extent that this holy and considerate friend takes up a place in your mind, the world with its vanities and trifles will leave you.

Peace of Soul and Humility

Nothing troubles us so much as self-love and self-regard. Should our hearts not grow soft with the sentiment we desire when we pray and with the interior sweetness we expect when we meditate, we are sorrowful; should we find some difficulty in doing good deeds, should some obstacle oppose our plans, we are in a dither to overcome it, and we labor anxiously. Why is this? Doubtless because we love our consolations, ease, and comfort. We want to pray as though we were bathing in comfort and to be virtuous as though we were eating dessert, all the while failing to look upon our sweet Jesus, who, prostrate on the ground, sweat blood and water from the distress of the extreme interior combat he underwent (Mark 14:35; Luke 22:44).

Self-love is one of the sources of our anxiety; the other is our high regard for ourselves. Why are we troubled to find that we have committed a sin or even an imperfection?

Because we thought ourselves to be something good, firm, and solid. And therefore, when we have seen the proof to the contrary, and have fallen on our faces in the dirt, we are troubled, offended, and anxious. If we understood ourselves, we would be astonished that we are ever able to remain standing. This is the other source of our anxiety: we want only consolations, and we are surprised to encounter our own misery, nothingness, and folly.

There are three things we must do to be at peace: have a pure intention to desire the honor and glory of God in all things; do the little that we can unto that end, following the advice of our spiritual father; and leave all the rest to God's care. Why should we torment ourselves if God is our aim and we have done all that we can? Why be anxious? What is there to fear? God is not so terrible to those who love him. He contents himself with little, for he knows how little we have. Our Lord is called the Prince of Peace in the Scriptures (Isaiah 9:6), and because he is the absolute master, he holds all things in peace. It is nevertheless true that before bringing peace to a place, he first brings war (cf. Matt. 10:34-36) by dividing the heart and soul from its most dear, familiar, and ordinary affections.

Now, when our Lord separates us from these passions, it seems that he burns our hearts alive, and we are embittered. The separation is so painful that it is barely possible for us to avoid fighting against it with all our soul. Peace is not lacking in the end when, although burdened by this distress, we keep our will resigned to our Lord, keep it nailed to God's good pleasure, and fulfill our duties courageously. We may take for example our Lord's agony in the garden, where, overwhelmed by interior and exterior bitterness, he nonetheless resigned himself peaceably to his Father's divine will, saying, "not my will, but thine be done" (Luke 22:42, Douay-Rheims). And he maintained this peace when admonishing three times the disciples who failed him (Matt. 26:40-45). At war with sin and suffering bitterly, he remained the Prince of Peace.

We can draw the following lessons from this consideration. The first is that we often mistakenly think that we have lost our peace when we are bitter. If we continue to deny ourselves and desire that everything should be done in accord with God's good pleasure, and if we fulfill our duties in spite of our bitterness, then we preserve our peace.

The second is that it is when we are suffering interiorly that God rips off the last bits of skin of the old man in order to renew in us the "new man that is made according to God" (cf. Eph. 4:22-24). And so we should never be disturbed by such sufferings or think that we are disgraced in our Lord's eyes.

Peace of Soul and Humility

The third is that all the thoughts that give us anxious and restless minds are not from God, who is the Prince of Peace; they are, therefore, temptations from the enemy, and we must reject them.

We must in all things remain at peace. Should interior or exterior pains afflict us, we must accept them peacefully. Should joys come our way, they must be received peacefully, without transport. If we must flee evil, we must do so calmly, without being disturbed; otherwise we may fall in our flight and give the enemy the chance to kill us. If there is good to be done, it must be done peacefully, or we will commit many faults through haste. Even penance must be done peacefully. "See," says the penitent, "that my great bitterness is in peace" (cf. Isa. 38:17).

As to humility, this virtue sees to it that we are neither troubled by our imperfections, nor in the habit of recalling those of others, for why should we be more perfect than our brothers? Why should we find it strange that others have imperfections since we ourselves have so many? Humility gives us a soft heart for the perfect and the imperfect: for the former out of reverence and for the latter out of compassion. Humility makes us accept pains with meekness, knowing that we deserve them, and good things with gratitude, knowing that we do not. Every day we ought to make some act of humility, or speak heartfelt words of humility, words that lower us to the level of a servant, and words that serve others, however modestly, either in our homes or in the world.

8

Christian Maturity

Ask our Lord that it should please him to console you with his blessing, to make your soul overflow with his holy love and with the sacred humility and meekness of his heart, which are never apart from his love, just as his love is never apart from them. Do not allow yourself to become angry or let yourself be surprised to see that your soul still has all the imperfections that you habitually confess. Even though you must reject and even detest them in order to amend your life, you must not oppose them with anger, but instead with courage and tranquillity, so that you will be able to make a solid and secure resolution to correct them. This resolution, made while you are at rest and with mature consideration, will help you to choose the true means of carrying it out, among which will be the moderation of your human affections. I do not counsel their abandonment, but only their moderation. Thus will you be able to find times in which you will be ready for prayer, for a little spiritual reading, for lifting your heart to God, and for recovering your self-possession and setting your heart at peace and in a posture of meekness and humility.

Compose your soul and let these resolutions sink deep within you. Above all, you must fight against a spirit of hatred for and discontent with your neighbor and abstain from an imperfection that we might not notice, but which is very damaging and which few people succeed in avoiding. When we censure our neighbor or complain about him—something we should do rarely—we never bring it to an end, but are always beginning again and endlessly repeating our complaints and grievances, which is a sign of a nettlesome heart that has not yet regained its health. Strong, robust hearts are sorrowful only about the most serious matters, and, even with respect to these they do not harbor resentment or let themselves be troubled.

9

☙

Oppressed in Conscience

The Savior of our souls has not given us an ardent desire to serve him without also giving us the means to do so. The heart of our Redeemer measures and adjusts everything that happens in the world to the advantage of those who desire to serve his divine love without reserve. It will surely come, that hour for which you long, on the day that sovereign providence has named in the secret of his mercy, and then it will come with thousands of secret consolations. Your soul will be open to his divine goodness, which will change your stones into water, your snake into a staff, the thorns in your heart into roses whose perfume will refresh your spirit with their sweetness. For it is true that our faults, while they are in our souls, are so many thorns, but upon being brought forth by self-accusation, they are changed into fragrant blossoms. Our malice keeps them within our hearts, and the goodness of the Holy Spirit expels them.

10

❧

Accepting God's Will

While taking a walk by yourself, or when you are alone at some other time, turn your eye to God's universal will and see how he wills all the works of his mercy and justice, in heaven and on earth and under the earth. Then with profound humility, accept, praise, and then bless this sovereign will, which is entirely holy, just, and beautiful.

Turn your eye next to God's particular will, by which he loves his own and accomplishes in them different works of consolation and tribulation. Ponder this a while, as you consider not only the variety of his consolations, but above all the trials suffered by the good. Then, with great humility, accept, praise, and bless the whole of this will.

Finally, consider this will in your own person, in all that befalls you for good or ill, and in all that can happen to you, except sin. Then, accept, praise, and bless all this, and declare your intention always to honor, cherish, and adore this sovereign will, confiding to his mercy and giving him your own life and those of your loved ones.

Conclude with an act of great confidence in his will, believing that he will do everything for us and for our happiness. After having made this exercise two or three times, you can shorten or vary it as you find best, but you should frequently recall it by short aspirations.

11

❧

The Visitation

What a lovely fragrance this beautiful lily brought to the whole house of Zechariah during the three months of her stay there. They were all busy with their various labors. She poured out honey and precious balm from her sacred lips with just a few, but most excellent words (cf. Song of Sol. 4:11). For what could she have shared with them other than that which she carried within herself? And she was carrying Jesus.

My God, I marvel that I am still so full of myself after having so often received Communion! O dear Jesus, be the child inside of us, so that we feel within and breathe forth nothing but you. Alas, you are so often within me; why am I so rarely in you? You enter into me; why am I so often outside of you? You are in my very self; why am I not in yours, to find there the great love of yours that transports our hearts?

12

⁊ᴗ

Maintaining Peace of Soul

None of us can become the master of our own soul in a short time or hold it firmly in our grasp from our very first steps. We should be content to gain small victories over our most unruly passions from time to time. We must bear with others, but first of all we must exercise forbearance toward ourselves and be patient with our own lack of perfection. Is it right for us to want to have interior peace without having first passed through the ordinary struggles of life?

Keep up the following practices. In the morning, prepare your soul to be at peace. Take care throughout the day to remember that resolution and to reaffirm it. Should you become disturbed, do not lose heart and do not be pained by it, but, having recognized the situation, calmly humble yourself before God and attempt to restore your mind to peace. Say to your soul: "Now, friend, we have made a misstep, let us proceed more carefully." And each time you fall, do the same thing. When you are at peace, make good use of the time, making as many acts of humility as you can, however insignificant they may be. For, as our Lord says, he who is faithful in little things will have great ones entrusted to him (Luke 16:10; Matt. 25:21-23). Above all, do not lose your courage, but be patient, watchful, and ready with a spirit of compassion. God will hold you in his hand, and if he lets you stumble, it will be only so that you realize that you would collapse entirely if he did not hold you, and thus to make you tighten your grip upon his hand.

13

Loving God

Does the love of God still rule in your heart? Does he hold the reins of all your affections and conquer all of your passions? Doubtless he does, but it is worth asking all the same, for the joy of hearing an answer. We so often ask people, "How are you doing? Are you well?" even though we can see for ourselves that they are in good health. Might we not find it agreeable if, without calling into doubt our virtue or our constancy, someone were to ask us, "Do you love God?" If we truly love him, we will be pleased to consider that fact often and will want frequently to speak to him and about him, and to spend time with him in the Blessed Sacrament. May he forever be the heart of our heart.

very powerful

14

❧

Bearing Jesus

We live in this world for one reason alone — to receive and to bear the sweet Jesus: on our tongues, by speaking of him; in our arms, by doing his good works; on our shoulders, by bearing his burden and his sufferings, both interior and exterior. O how happy are they who carry him gently and faithfully! I have truly carried him on my tongue every day. And I have carried him to Egypt, it seems to me, inasmuch as in the sacrament of confession I have heard a great number of penitents who with great confidence have addressed themselves to me in order to receive him into their sinful souls. Oh, may it please God to wish to remain there!

There is but one great word of our salvation: Jesus! May we be able, at least once, to say this sacred name with all our heart. What a balm it pours out upon all of the powers of our soul. How happy we shall be to have nothing in our understanding but Jesus, nothing in our memory but Jesus, nothing in our will but Jesus, nothing in our imagination but Jesus. Jesus will be everywhere in us, and we will be all in him. Let us attempt it by saying his name as often as we can. Although we can but stutter now, in the end we shall say it well.

15

❦

Bearing Our Crosses

Nothing can bring us a more profound peace in this world than to look upon our Lord in all the afflictions that befell him from his birth to his death. In his life we see so much calumny, poverty, dependence, pain, torment, injury, and every sort of bitterness that, in reflecting on them, we see that we are wrong to call our little trials afflictions and pains and to think that we need more patience in order to endure them, inasmuch as a little drop of modesty is all we really need to enable us to bear with what happens to us. Your soul has all these movements of sadness, astonishment, and anxiety because it is not yet sufficiently grounded in the love of the Cross and in resignation to God's will.

A heart that greatly respects and loves Jesus Christ crucified loves his death, pain, torment, insults, hunger, thirst, and shame, and, when some small participation in them comes, such a heart rejoices and embraces it lovingly. Every day you should bring to mind the sufferings our Lord endured for our redemption—not while at prayer, but at another time, such as when taking a walk—and consider how good it is for you to participate in them. Find out how to do so, that is, how to frustrate your desires, and especially your most just and legitimate desires; and then, with a great love for the Passion and Cross of our Lord, cry out with St. Andrew, "O blessed Cross, so beloved to my Savior, when will you receive me in your arms?"

16

❦

Facing Temptation

Your temptations have returned, and although you have not said a word of consent to them, still they oppress you. You do not consent to them, and that is good, but you fear them too much. They would not be able to harm you if you did not fear them.

You are too sensitive to these temptations. You love the faith and wish that not a single contrary thought would come to you, and as soon as one does, you are sad and troubled. You are too jealous of this purity of faith, and it seems that everything spoils it. But you should let the winds blow and not think that the whirling leaves are so many clashing armies.

I was recently near some beehives, and some of the bees landed on my face. I wanted to shoo them away with my hand. "No," said the beekeeper, "have no fear, and do not touch them; then they will not sting you. But should you touch them, you will indeed be stung." I believed him and was not stung by a single one.

Believe me in turn: do not fear temptations, and do not touch them, and they will not offend you. Pass them by, and take no interest in them. In the end, no human remedy has proven capable of healing this injury, which causes you a pain that you must wisely transmute into a perpetual penance. This is a blow from divine providence, so that you may have cause for patience and mortification. O what treasures will you be able to store up by this means! You must persevere and live as a true rose among thorns.

17

The Burden of Work

You are submerged by a flood of troubles that the size of your household places on your shoulders. You must, then, call upon our Lord all the more and beg for his holy help, so that the work you must do will be agreeable to him and so that you will embrace it for his honor and glory. Our days are few (cf. Job 14:1), and consequently our labor cannot be overlong. By means of a little patience, we will get through it with honor and contentment, for we have no greater consolation at the end of the day than to have worked hard and shouldered its pains.

18

❧

Too Busy to Pray

The length of your prayers should be measured by the amount of your work, and inasmuch as it has pleased our Lord to place you in the kind of life in which you are perpetually distracted, you must accustom yourself to making short prayers, but you must also make them so habitual that you will never omit them except upon the rarest occasions.

In the morning, when you rise, you should bend your knees before God to adore him, make the Sign of the Cross, and ask him for his blessing for the entire day; this can be accomplished in the amount of time it takes to say one or two Our Fathers.

If you go to Mass, it will suffice for you to hear it devoutly and attentively. In the evening, before the meal or just after it, you can easily find the time to make a few fervent prayers, throwing yourself before our Lord for as long as it takes to say one Our Father—for there can hardly be an occasion that holds you so bound that you cannot tear away such a little bit of leisure.

At night, before retiring, you can, while you do other things and wherever you may be, pass under review what you have done during the day, in outline, and then, as you go to bed, throw yourself on your knees and ask God's pardon for the faults you have committed, and pray him to watch over you and give you his blessing. This you can do in short compass, in about the time of a Hail Mary.

Above all, during the day, you should bring your heart back to God and say to him a few brief words of fidelity and love.

19

&

Perseverance in Worship

You should firmly believe that you harbor no lasting desires contrary to the will of God — that is, desires for venial sin — even though certain imperfections and bad inclinations surprise you from time to time.

Do not cease receiving Communion. No longer be in doubt, but employ your heart in being faithful to the exercise of poverty amid wealth, meekness and calm amid clamor, and resignation to all that can befall you in God's providence. When we have God, what else can we possibly need?

It is better for you to assist at Mass every day than not to do so on the pretext of having more time to pray at home. It is better not only because the real presence of the humanity of our Lord cannot be replaced by his presence in our minds, but also because the Church strongly desires that we attend Mass. We can consider this desire as advice that to follow is a kind of obedience when we can do so rightly and, by our good example, be of use to others.

20

❧

Parents and Teachers

We must suffer much from children while they are young; they sometimes even hurt the one who nourishes them. The words of the great apostle should serve us as a maxim: "in season and out of season ... be unfailing in patience and in teaching" (2 Tim. 4:2). He puts patience first, as being the more necessary and that without which teaching is in vain. He wants us to suffer those who annoy us. Let us continue to cultivate well; there is no ground so ungrateful that a laborer's love cannot cause it to bear fruit.

21

❧

A Devout Life

You wish to have a devout and peaceful spirit, which is not a small thing to wish for. The virtue of devotion is nothing other than a general inclination and readiness of the spirit to do what is pleasing to God. It is that opening of the heart of which David spoke: "I will run in the way of your commandments when you have opened up my heart" (Ps. 119:32, following de Sales's reading of the Vulgate). Those who are simply upright men and women walk in the way of the Lord, but the devout run along it, and when they are very devout, they fly. Here are a few rules that you must follow in order to be truly devout.

You must before all things observe the general commandments of God and of the Church, which are established for all faithful Christians, and without which it is not possible to have any devotion. Beyond the general commandments, you must carefully keep the particular commandments that relate to your vocation. Whoever fails to do so, even if he were to raise the dead, will fall into a state of sin and, if he die, be damned. For instance, bishops are commanded to visit their flock, to teach, reprove, and console them. If I were to remain at prayer throughout the week, fast my whole life, and yet neglect these prescribed duties, I would die. If a person in the married state were to work a miracle but not fulfill the duties of marriage or care for his children, he would be "worse than an unbeliever" (1 Tim. 5:8).

These, then, are the two kinds of commandments that must be carefully kept as the foundation of all devotion. Yet the virtue of devotion does not consist in merely observing them, but in observing them promptly and willingly. The following considerations will help you to acquire this readiness.

The first is that God so wishes it, and we exist to do his will. Alas, every day we pray that "his will be done," and yet when it comes to our doing it, how difficult it is! We offer ourselves to God so often, we say to him, "Lord, I am yours" (cf. Ps. 119:94), and then when he wants to make use of us, we are so cowardly! How can we call ourselves his if we do not want to bend our will to his?

The second consideration is to think about the nature of God's sweet, gracious, and mild commandments, not only the general ones, but still more those pertaining to our vocations. What could cause them to annoy us? Nothing, except our own will, which wants to reign no matter the cost. We desire things when they are not commanded and reject the same things when they are. From out of a hundred thousand delicious fruits, Eve chose the single one that was forbidden to her, and no doubt she would not have done so had it been permissible. In a word, we wish to serve God, but according to our will, not his. To the extent to which we have less self will, we shall more easily observe the will of God.

22

❦

Blessed Joseph

Let us consider the greatness of this blessed saint, whom our hearts love because he nourished the Love of our hearts and the heart of our love. "Do good, O LORD, to those who are good, and to those who are upright in their hearts!" (Ps. 125:4). From these words we can conclude that this saint was good and upright of heart, for the Lord did so much good to him, having given him his Mother and his Son. With these two treasures, he could have made the angels envy him and defied all heaven to try to equal him in his possessions. For what is there that the angels have that is comparable to the Queen of Angels? And is there a God greater than our God?

23

❧

Imperfection

Do not examine with great care to find whether you are in a state of perfection. And here are two reasons: first, it is fruitless, inasmuch as even if we were the most perfect in the world, we would never know or understand it, but instead would always consider ourselves to be imperfect. Our examination should never be for the sake of finding out whether we are imperfect, because that is something we ought never to doubt.

From thence it follows that we should never be surprised to find ourselves imperfect. Nor should we be saddened by it, for the remedy is at hand. We should either humble ourselves, for thus we repair our defects, or gently amend ourselves, because this work is the reason we are left imperfect. And although it is inexcusable to fail to amend oneself, it is excusable if we fail to do so perfectly, for we ought not to take imperfections to be sins.

The other reason is that such an examination, when made with anxiety and confusion, is a waste of time. Those who busy themselves with it resemble soldiers who, to prepare for battle, engage in many tournaments and other excesses such that, when it comes to the day of trial, they find themselves worn out; or like singers who make themselves hoarse by too much practice. The spirit gets worn out with so great and continual an examination, and when it comes time, it can no longer act.

"If your eye is sound," said the Lord, "you whole body will be full of light" (Matt. 6:22). Simplify your judgment. Do not turn things over and over, but instead proceed directly and with confidence. In this world there are only two things: you and God. Nothing else should disturb you, unless God should so command it, and then only to that extent. Keep your sight fixed upon God and yourself. You will never see God without seeing his goodness, or yourself without seeing your misery, and you will see that his goodness answers to your misery, and that your misery is the object of his goodness and mercy.

24

Confidence amid Tribulation

There is no doubt that these various unpleasant happen-
ings have been a great trial for you. But in what, when, and
how can we bear witness to the true fidelity that we owe
to our Lord if not amid tribulation, opposition, and during
those times when we are unsettled within? This life is such
that we must eat bitter herbs more often than honey, but
the One for whose sake we have resolved to persevere in
holy patience, despite so many kinds of opposition, will
give us the consolation of his Holy Spirit in due season.
"Do not throw away your confidence," says the apostle
(Heb. 10:35). This confidence that restores our vigor will
allow you to suffer and withstand with great courage any
battle you face, no matter how grave.

25

A Strong Heart

The truth must be confessed: we are but poor souls who can barely accomplish any good. But God, who is infinitely good, contents himself with our small strides and is pleased by the strengthening of our heart (Ps. 10:17). What does it mean to strengthen our heart? According to the holy Word, "God is greater than our hearts" (1 John 3:20), and our heart is greater than the whole world. When our heart, alone in its meditation, makes itself ready for the service it owes to God—that is to say, when it makes its plans to serve God, to honor him, to serve our neighbor, to mortify the exterior and interior senses, and other such good purposes—this is when the heart works miracles. It gathers its forces and disposes our actions to a most admirable and eminent degree of perfection.

If we consider the greatness of God and his immense goodness and dignity, we will want to attempt, for his sake, great spiritual works. We will want to offer him a mortified flesh that does not rebel, an attentiveness to prayer impervious to distraction, a way of life so meek that it lacks all bitterness, and a humility entirely purged of vanity.

All this is well and good: these are the efforts we should make. And we must do still more in order to serve God according to our duty. Beyond all this, we must be truthful. For we see our imperfections, how we fail to subdue the flesh entirely, how we succumb to distraction, and so forth. Must we, then, be anxious, troubled, and cast down? No, certainly not. Must we somehow redouble our efforts so that we actually arrive at perfection? In truth, no. In order to walk aright, we must apply ourselves to the path that lies before us and to the tasks of this day. We must not pretend that we are about to accomplish the work of the last day before we have finished the work of the first.

26

❧

John the Baptist

John the Baptist knew our Lord from his mother's womb, trembling for joy at his presence and at the sound of Mary's voice, and thus bearing witness to the happiness he would have to see him, hear him, and speak with him. Nevertheless, he was deprived of all that; the Scriptures testify to only two times that he spoke to him. Knowing that this divine Savior was preaching and sharing himself with everyone in Judea, John remained solitary in the nearby desert, without daring to come to see him in person, even though he saw him spiritually every day. Was there ever a mortification equal to this one: to be so close to his only and sovereign Love, and, for love of him, to remain without either seeing or hearing him? And we do the same thing when we are near to the Sacrament where Jesus is, for there we taste him only in spirit, just as St. John did.

27

❧

Ordered Desires

You are probably right in thinking that the true source of your woes is that you have a multitude of desires that cannot all be satisfied. A variety of dishes always burdens the digestion and, if the stomach is weak, will ruin it. When the soul that has left behind concupiscence and been purged of evil and worldly affections encounters spiritual and holy objects, it hungrily fills itself with so many and such pressing desires that it is overcome by them. Ask for help from our Lord and from the spiritual fathers who know you and thus will know what remedies will help you. If you begin to pursue even a few of these desires, they will continue to multiply and will trouble your mind in such a way that you will not know how to disentangle yourself.

The thing must be dealt with purposefully. But according to what order? You must begin with tangible and exterior things, which are the ones most in your power. For example, in order for you to accomplish some common and menial tasks around the house out of humility, it is not necessary for you first to have the desire to serve the sick for the love of our Lord; the household duties are fundamental, and failure in them renders every other work suspect. You ought to bestir yourself to these works; the occasion to perform them will not be wanting. To do them is entirely in your power, and, moreover, you ought to do them, for it would be vain to desire to perform works that are beyond your power or far from your home, while you were neglecting these that are before you. Faithfully act upon your desires to exercise charity, humility, and the other virtues, and you will see that all will be well. Mary Magdalene first had to wash the feet of our Lord, then kiss them and dry them, before conversing with him heart to heart in meditation, and she poured out ointment over his body prior to pouring out the balm of her contemplation of his divinity.

It is good to desire much, but you must order your desires and bring them forth each according to its season and your ability. We prune vines and trees so that there will be sap sufficient for much fruit, so that their natural power will not be dedicated to the overabundant production of leaves. If we allow our desires to multiply, our soul may be content merely to desire and fail to attend to the works themselves, the very least accomplishment of which is, in general, more useful than the storing up of wishes to do things that are beyond our power. God desires from us more fidelity to the little things that he places in our power than ardor for great things that do not depend upon us.

28

Impatience or Self-Love

This impatience of which you speak, is it truly impatience, or is it not the sign of your nature recoiling? Since you call it impatience, it may be taken to be such, but your letters also show that you have a heart that attaches itself strongly to those things that are means toward what you greatly desire. Now, what you most greatly desire is to love God and to perform various exercises and practices that increase that love. It seems, however, that you are strongly attached to these practices and wish that everything could be reduced to them. This is why you are anxious when others prevent you from employing them or bring you distractions.

The remedy will be for you to make an effort to banish anxiety; God wants you to serve him as you are, and by the exercises and virtuous deeds that accord with your state in life. And in addition to persuading yourself of this truth, you must also make yourself to love your state in life and its duties, and to love them tenderly, for the sake of the One who has willed it thus. But you see, this must not be a passing thought, it must be a consideration that remains in the very front of your heart. Over time, by continual recollection and attention, this truth will become enjoyable to your spirit. And believe me, anything contrary to this advice is nothing other than self-love.

29

In the Desert

We must not spend too much time thinking and examining ourselves about the origin of our spiritual dryness. If it comes from our faults, we must not become anxious, but with a very simple and gentle humility we must reject them and then place ourselves in the hands of our Lord so that he can help us to carry the burden, or pardon us, according to his good pleasure. We must not be so curious as to wish to know whence the different states of our lives proceed. We must submit ourselves to everything that God ordains and let the rest be.

30

Christian Liberty

Before all things we ask God that his "name be hallowed," that his "kingdom come," and that his "will be done on earth as it is in heaven." These desires represent the true spirit of liberty, for, provided that the name of God be sanctified, his majesty reign in us, and his will be done, we need nothing more. He whose heart is thus free is not attached to consolations but receives afflictions with all the meekness that the flesh allows. While the desire for consolations is not eradicated, he is not attached to them. He is detached even from spiritual exercises, to the degree that should illness or accident prevent them, he is not full of regrets. I do not say that he fails to love them, only that he is not attached to them. And he hardly ever loses his joy, because no privation can sadden the one whose heart is attached to nothing. I do not say that he never loses it, but that he quickly regains it.

Christian Liberty

The effects of this liberty are a great sweetness of spirit and a great mildness and condescension to everything that is not sinful or a threat of sin. This is the temperament that is ready for the exercise of all the virtues.

This liberty has two contrary vices: instability and constraint, that is, dissoluteness and servitude. Instability of spirit or dissoluteness is a certain excess of liberty by which one wants to change his state in life and duties without reason and without divining God's will. At the least provocation, the restless one changes his plans and way of life, and every little event gives him occasion to set aside his rule and his praiseworthy habits. In this way, his heart is dissipated and is lost, and he is like an orchard open on all sides, whose fruits are no longer for the owner, but instead for every passerby.

Constraint or servitude is a certain lack of liberty by which the spirit is burdened or annoyed or angered when it cannot carry out its own plans, even when able to choose something better. Here is an example. My plan is to meditate every day in the morning. If I am unstable or dissolute, the least occasion will suffice for me to skip it in the evening: for a dog that will not let me sleep or for a letter that I must write. On the contrary, if I have the spirit of constraint or servitude, I will not leave off my meditation even if someone who is sick has great need of my assistance.

31

Perseverance in Prayer

You should not reproach yourself if you are not finding consolation in meditation, but proceed gently and with humility and patience, not in any way injuring your spirit. Make use of a book when you find your mind to be weary, that is to say, read a bit and then meditate, and then read again for a bit and then meditate, until you reach the end of your half hour. Teresa of Avila made this her practice in the beginning, and she tells us that it did her great good. Keep as your rule the truth that the grace of meditation cannot be won by any efforts of our minds; what is required is a gentle and very affectionate perseverance, full of humility.

32

Judge Your Feelings

Feelings, even pleasant ones, can be from our enemy or from our friend, that is, from the evil one or from the one who is all goodness. Now, we can discern whence they come by certain signs, of which here are a few that will suffice to guide you.

When we do not rest in them, but when we make use of them only for recreation in order afterward to fulfill with a greater constancy the duties and work that God has confided to us, that is a good sign. God sometimes gives us consolations for this reason. He condescends to our infirmity. He sees that our taste for spiritual things has dulled, and he gives us a little gravy, but only to prompt us to desire the nourishing meat. It is therefore a good indication when we do not tarry in the enjoyment of our feelings, for when the evil one gives us certain feelings, he wants us to rest in them; when we do, when we eat only gravy, our spiritual stomachs become weakened and spoiled.

Secondly, the right sort of feelings do not make us at all proud. Our understanding must remain entirely humble and submissive to God, recognizing that Caleb and Joshua would never have brought word to the Israelites of the delights of the Promised Land had they not thought them to be in need of having their courage stirred. If, instead of puffing itself up, our understanding recognizes its own weakness and lovingly humiliates itself before God, then we will realize that these feelings are given to us as a reward and protection.

These good feelings do not leave us weakened, but strengthened, not afflicted, but consoled. The bad ones, however, bring a certain transport when they come and leave us full of anguish when they depart. Good feelings, when they depart, recommend to us the pursuit of virtue in their absence; indeed it is for our growth in virtue that they are given to us. The bad ones suggest that when they depart, virtue does too, and they leave us dispirited. In brief, good feelings do not call for love, but only for us to love the One who sends them, while the bad ones want us to love them above all things. Good feelings impel us to seek virtue; bad ones to seek feelings themselves.

33

☙

Be Patient

My friend, we will soon be in heaven, and there we shall see what little account are the affairs of this world and how little it matters whether they are done or not. Now it is true that they do press upon us as if they were great things. When we were children, how earnestly did we build little houses and castles out of bits of wood and tile and mud! And if someone were to knock them down, we would be upset and teary. Yet now we know quite well that all those things were of little moment. One day it will be the same in heaven; we will see that the things we cared about in the world were the playthings of children.

I do not wish to discourage you from employing the care that you ought with these little baubles and nothings, for God has entrusted them to us in this world. Let us do our childish things, for we are indeed children, but let us not bring ruin upon ourselves by doing them. And if someone knocks down our little houses, we should not torment ourselves. For when the evening comes and we must die, these little houses will not serve at all; it is then that we must go up to the house of our Father (cf. Ps. 122:1). Take care of your affairs faithfully, but do so knowing that you have no more worthy affair than your soul's path to salvation.

Be patient with all, but especially with yourself. Do not trouble yourself about your imperfections. Always have the courage to pick yourself back up and begin again every day, for there is no better path to success in the spiritual life than always to begin again and never to think that you have done enough.

34

Pardon Your Heart

We must always desire to carry out our spiritual exercises well and with precision, both prayer and the exercise of the virtues, and we must never be troubled, anxious, or surprised if we fail to do so. Our desires depend upon our fidelity, which should always be total and yet should grow from day to day; our failures are caused by our infirmity, which we will never be able to leave behind during this mortal life. When we have committed some fault, we should immediately examine our heart and ask ourselves whether we retain a lively and thorough resolution to serve God.

One hopes for a heart that would rather suffer a thousand deaths than fail to keep this resolution. We reprove our heart: "Why, then, are you hesitating now? Why are you so cowardly?" And we make our excuse: "I was taken by surprise, and I hardly know how it happened, but now I am again thinking of my resolution." The heart must be pardoned. It is not through infidelity that it failed, but through infirmity. It must be corrected gently and calmly, that it not be brought to anger or further trouble. We should say to it: "My heart, my friend, in the name of God, be courageous. Let us walk together, taking care as we go, lifting ourselves up to our help, to our God." And, we must be charitable toward our soul, not taking it to task severely, provided we see that it is not offending purposefully. Do you not see that in treating it this way, we practice a holy humility?

35

A Time of Depression

A melancholy humor has overcome you for a time, and, from being sorrowful, you have become anxious. Do not let yourself be anxious. Do not lose your peace. Even though it seems to you that you do everything without any savor, feeling, or strength, continue to embrace our crucified Lord, and give him your heart and consecrate your mind to him with your affections just as they are, however languid they may be.

Blessed Angela of Foligni said that our Lord revealed to her that there was no kind of good deed more pleasing to him than the ones we force ourselves to do, that is to say, the ones that a firmly resolved will accomplishes in spite of the languor of the flesh and the repugnance of our lower selves and in the face of dryness, sorrow, and interior dereliction. How happy you will be if you are faithful amid the crosses that present themselves to you, faithful to the

One who loved you so faithfully "unto death, even death on a cross" (Phil. 2:8).

36

࿎

Our Daily Bread

You say that you do nothing when you pray. Yet what do you desire beyond what you are doing, which is presenting to God your nothingness and misery?

The most effective appeal that beggars make is simply to place their open wounds and needs before us. Yet, you say, sometimes you do not even accomplish that, and you remain like a phantom or a statue. But even this is no small thing. In the palaces of princes and kings, statues are placed for no other purpose than for the prince to look upon them. Content yourself to be in God's presence in that way; he will bring the statue to life when it pleases him to do so.

Trees require sunlight to bear fruit. Some do so earlier, others later, some annually, others only every third year, and none of them bears the same way as the others. We should be happy to be able to remain in the presence of

Roses Among Thorns

God and be content that he will make us bear fruit sooner or later, either daily or now and then, according to his good pleasure.

37

❧

Oppressed by Pain

Let us practice that holy resignation and pure love of our Lord that is never as perfect as it is amid suffering. To love God while eating desserts: little children would do as much. But to love him while eating bitter herbs: that is the victory of a loving fidelity. Even St. Peter had enough courage to say "Long live Jesus" on Mount Tabor; but to say "Long live Jesus" on Mount Calvary: that belonged only to our Lord's Mother and to the beloved disciple, who was left as her child. We must pray for that holy resignation so that God can shape our hearts into a fitting place for him to dwell and reign eternally. What difference does it make if he does that work with the hammer or scissors or a needle, provided he do it according to his pleasure?

Your sufferings have been steadily mounting: our Lord is allowing you to participate in his holy Cross and is crowning you with his crown of thorns. Your pain is so great that you cannot keep your mind upon the labors that our Lord undertook for your sake. It is not necessary that you do so, provided you simply lift your heart to the Savior as often as you can while accomplishing these actions.

First, accept your trials from his hand, as though he were laying them upon you himself. Second, offer to suffer still more. Third, swear, by the merits of his suffering, to accept small inconveniences in union with the pain that he suffered on the Cross. Fourth, tell him that you will not only accept, but even love and cherish these troubles because they have been sent by so good and gentle a hand. Fifth, call upon the martyrs and the servants of God who rejoice in heaven because they were so greatly afflicted in this world. There is no danger in desiring to be healed; indeed, you must carefully work to that end, because God, who sent you this suffering, is also the author of all healing. Seek help, but with the resignation that should his divine majesty wish the illness to conquer you, you will accept it, and if he wishes you to be healed, you will bless him. How happy you will be if you keep yourself humbly in God's hand.

A Prayer for a Time of Suffering

O Lord Jesus, by your incomparable sadness and by the unparalleled desolation that seized your divine

*heart on the Mount of Olives and on the Cross, and
by the desolation of your dear Mother when she lost
you, be our joy, or at least be our strength, now while
your Cross and Passion are so closely joined to our
hearts.*

38

⋆

The Envy of the Angels

Why do the angels envy us? Truly, it is for no other reason than that we are able to suffer for our Lord, while they have never suffered anything for him. St. Paul, who was lifted to heaven amid the joys of paradise, did not count himself blessed except because of his infirmities, and in the Cross of our Lord (2 Cor. 12:3-10; Gal. 6:14). When you suffer in your body, speak the same words as the apostle: "Henceforth let no man trouble me; for I bear on my body the marks of Jesus" (Gal. 6:17). Suffering borne well will carry you closer to heaven than if you were the healthiest person in the world! Paradise is a mountain up which we climb better with a body broken and injured than with one healthy and whole.

39

A Quiet Life

How happy are the bees. They leave their hive only to gather nectar for their honey, congregate only for their common work, are busy only unto that end. Their ordered bustle is directed to filling their houses with the aromatic labor of honey and wax making. They are much happier than the libertine wasps and flies, who dash around at whim to things that are as unclean as they are undignified and seem to exist only to bother the rest of the animals and to cause them pain. They are everywhere ferreting about, sucking and stinging as long as summer and autumn last, and when winter comes, they find themselves without shelter, larder, or life. But from the nobility of their work, our chaste bees have gained a most suitable shelter, agreeable provisions, and a contented life amid the profits of their earlier labors.

In the same way, those souls who love the Savior and who, according to the Gospel (John 6:1-15) follow him into the desert, find a more delicious feast there upon the grass and the flowers than is ever enjoyed by those who choose the lavish array of Ahasuerus, where abundance suffocates joy (Esther 1:3-8).

40

٭

The Ascension

Our Savior has risen into heaven, where he lives and reigns, and he desires that one day we should live and reign there with him. What a triumph in heaven, and what sweetness upon the earth! Oh, that our hearts were where our treasure is and that we should live in heaven, where is our true life! (Col. 3:4). How lovely heaven is, now that the Savior is its sun and his side a flowing fountain of love from which the blessed drink to their content. Each sees himself there, his name written in letters of love, that love alone can read, and that love alone was able to write. Shall our names be written there? We may trust that they will, for even if our hearts do not have love, at least they desire to love and thus have the beginning of love.

Is not the sacred name of Jesus written in our hearts? We must hope that our name also will be written on God's heart. What happiness shall be ours when we see those divine letters spelling out our own eternal blessedness! An eternity of good things awaits us, one in which everything pales in comparison to the invariable love of this great God who reigns there. We are so full of contradiction: to have sentiments so pure but actions so sullied. For truly paradise could be filled with the pains of hell, provided the love of God were there, and if the fires of hell were a fire of love, its torments would be desirable. Every heavenly delight would be true nothingness beside this reigning love. So how can it be that we do not love in return? Let us pray and work and humble ourselves, invoking this love upon us.

41

❦

Not into Temptation

You must not believe that temptations against the Faith and the Church come from God. Darkness, weakness, prostration, abandonment, loss of vigor, an interior void, a bitterness in the interior mouth capable of souring the world's sweetest wines, yes — but suggestions of blasphemy, infidelity, unbelief, no: these do not come from our good God (James 1:13). He is too pure to have such a purpose.

Do you know what God is doing in all of this? He allows the evil maker of these sordid things to display them to us so that by our disdain for them we might testify to our affection for divine things. It is the devil who prowls around our mind (1 Pet. 5:8), seeking a way to enter, an open door. He did the same with Job, with St. Antony, with St. Catherine of Siena, and with many other good souls. Should we lose our temper because of him? Let him lurk around while we hold all the ports of entry tightly closed. He will eventually desist; if he does not do so willingly, God will force him to. It is a good sign that he should make so much noise without, for it means that he is not within your will. Take heart. I say it with great feeling and in Jesus Christ: take heart. As long as we can say resolutely—even if we do not feel it—"Long live Jesus!" then there will be nothing to fear.

42

St. Peter in Chains

Our great St. Peter, awakened from his sleep by the angel: how many consolations there are in the story of his deliverance (Acts 12:3-11). His soul was transported to such a degree that he did not know whether he was dreaming. May our angel touch our side today to awaken us into a loving attentiveness to God, to deliver us from the chains of self-love and to consecrate us once and for all to this heavenly love so that we might say, "Now I know that God sent his angel and rescued me."

How happy was our dear St. Peter! It was to show his love that our Lord asked him, "Peter, do you love me?" It was not that he doubted, but instead for the sake of the great pleasure that he took from often hearing us say, and say again, and insist that we love him.

Do we love our sweet Savior? Oh, he knows full well that if we do not love him, we at least desire to love him.

Now, if we love him, let us feed his sheep and his lambs, for that is the mark of faithful love. With what shall we feed these dear little sheep? With love itself, for they either do not love at all, or they live upon love. Between love and death there is no middle. We must die or love, for he who loves not, as St. John says, remains in death (1 John 3:14).

Our Lord said to St. Peter, "When you were young, you fastened your own belt and walked where you would; but when you are old, you will stretch out your hands, and another will fasten your belt for you and carry you where you do not wish to go" (cf. John 21:18). Young apprentices in the love of God fasten their own belts. They take up the mortifications that seem good to them; they choose their penances and make up their own minds about God's will. But the old masters of the craft allow themselves to be bound by others and submit to the yoke imposed upon them, and travel down paths upon which they do not wish to travel. In spite of the resistance of their inclinations, they voluntarily allow themselves to be governed against their will and say that they would rather obey than make an offering, and this is how they glorify God, by crucifying not only their flesh, but also their spirit.

43

❧

A Time of Fear

What words can oppose the flood of thoughts troubling your heart? Do not attempt to stop them; that will only make the pain worse. Do not try to conquer the temptations; the effort will only make them stronger. Disdain them, and do not dwell on them. Bring to mind an image of Jesus Christ crucified and say, "Here is my hope; here is the flowing fountain of my happiness. Here is the heart of my soul and the soul of my heart." Hear our Lord say to Abraham and to you: "Be not afraid; I am your protector" (cf. Gen. 15:1). What is it that you seek upon the earth other than your God? And you already possess him.

Be firm in your resolutions. Stay in the boat. Let the storm come. While Jesus lives, you will not die. He is sleeping, but he will awaken to calm the storm at the right time (Matt. 8:24-26). St. Peter, the Scriptures tell us, saw the great storm and was afraid, and as soon as he was afraid, he began to sink and drown. Whereupon he cried out, "O Lord, save me!" And our Lord took him by the hand and said to him, "O man of little faith, why did you doubt?" (Matt. 14:29-31). See this great apostle: he walked with dry feet upon the water, protected from wind and wave, but the fear of the wind and the wave would have killed him had not his Master relieved him.

Fear is a greater evil than evil itself. O you of little faith: what is it you fear? Do not be afraid. You are walking on water, amid wind and wave, but you are with Jesus. What is there to fear? If fear takes hold of you, cry out strongly, "O Lord, save me!" He will hold out a hand to you. Hold on tight, and go forward with joy.

44

❦

The Baptist amid the Thorns

Think upon the rose. It represents the glorious St. John, whose ruby-red charity is more vibrant than the rose, which he nevertheless resembles because he lived amid the thorns of many mortifications. Consider how this great man had engraved in his heart the holy Virgin and her child from the day of her visitation, on which he — first of mortals — sensed how worthy of love were the Mother of this child and the child of this Mother.

Nothing beyond this Mother and this child should occupy our hearts. May the glorious and divine Jesus always live and reign in our minds, in the arms of his holy Mother, as upon a blossoming throne.

Here is a spiritual bouquet made of two lilies and one rose, one born in the other, and both of them blessing, with the scent of their sweetness and the perfection of their beauty, the rose of their hearts, which, by a perfect piercing mortification, lives stripped and bereft of every other thing for their sake.

45

God's Vigilance

You are persevering in your desire to serve our Lord, even though you are surrounded by snares and obstacles. If you are faithful along this journey, you will have a consolation greater than every challenge. You are living amid the clamor of the world, which can divert the holy attention that you wish to give to God. Try to make this trial useful to your spiritual progress. We have no reward without victory, no victory without war. Take courage, therefore, and transform your pain—which has no cure—into an occasion for virtue.

Look often to our Lord, who watches over you, poor little creature that you are, and sees you surrounded by labors and distractions. He is sending you help and is blessing your affliction. With this in mind, you should patiently and meekly bear annoyances for the love of him who permits them only for your benefit. Lift your heart to God, call upon his aid, and make your chief consolation be the happiness of belonging to him. All of the causes of your displeasure will seem slight when you know that you have such a friend, so great a support, and so excellent a refuge.

46

The Assumption

How lovely is this Dawn of the everlasting day, who, carried into heaven, seems only to grow in the blessedness of her incomparable glory. May the scents of eternal sweetness wafting upon those who love her always fill our hearts, and may we always rejoice in the blessings prepared for the souls of her faithful ones. We are the unworthy children of this glorious Mother, the star of the sea, "fair as the moon, bright as the sun" (Song of Sol. 6:10). Let us attempt great things under her protection, for she will reward even our paltry tenderness with success. In the Song of Solomon, she says "refresh me with apples" (2:5); we should willingly give her our heart—what other apple could she desire from us? Then God will give us the grace of being face-to-face with her one day, in the benediction of the divine love.

47

A Spiritual Vintage

Just as wine is made by pressing the grapes, so we make a spiritual vintage by pressing upon God's grace and his promises. To press upon God's grace, we must multiply our prayers by brief but lively movements of our hearts. To press upon his promises, we must multiply our works of charity, for it is to these that God has joined his promises. "I was sick and you visited me," he said (Matt. 25:36).

Each thing has its season: in one we press the grapes, and in another we bring the vintage forth from the cellar, but we must press, and do so carefully and without anxiety. On the Cross, there is but one grape, although it is worth more than thousands. How much nourishment have holy souls found there, by thinking upon the graces and virtues that our Savior showed forth to the world. Make a good harvest of your earthly labors, and they will serve you as a ladder to climb to spiritual ones.

A Spiritual Vintage

St. Francis loved the lambs and the sheep because they reminded him of his dear Savior, and we ought to love our work in gathering the harvest and making temporal wine, not only because these tasks correspond to the requirement that we earn our bread each day, but also, and much more so, because they lift our minds to a spiritual vintage. Keep your heart full of love, but with a love that is mild, peaceful, and firm. Consider your faults, as well as those of others, with more humility than severity. Live joyously, for you are entirely dedicated to an everlasting joy, which is God himself, who wishes to live and reign forever from the very heart of your heart.

48

Complaining

With regard to those matters that are troubling your heart, you should be able to discern easily which of them have a remedy and which do not. Where there is a remedy, you must labor to apply it gently and peaceably. When there is none, you must endure them as a mortification that our Lord sends you in order to train you and to make you entirely his own. Take care not to allow yourself to complain, but instead constrain your heart to suffer in tranquillity. If some sudden surge of impatience should come over you, restore your heart to peacefulness and meekness. God indeed loves those souls who are tossed about by the storms and waves of the world, provided they receive their travails from his hand and, like mighty warriors, endeavor to remain faithful amid the fray.

49

❧

Beautiful Devotion

In order to be devout, not only must we want to do the will of God, we must do it joyfully. If I were not a bishop, yet knew what I know, I would not want to be one. But being one, not only am I obliged to do what this annoying office requires, but I must do it joyfully, and I must take delight in it and accept it. To do so is to follow St. Paul's saying, "in whatever state each was called, there let him remain with God" (1 Cor. 7:24).

We must carry not the crosses of others, but our own. And this means that each of us must "deny himself" (Matt. 16:24), that is to say, to deny his own will. "I want to do this; I would be better there than here": we are tempted by such thoughts. Our Lord knows what he is about. Let us do his will and remain where he has placed us.

Not only should you be devout and love the devout life, but you should be making that life beautiful to behold.

Roses Among Thorns

Now, it will be beautiful to the extent to which it is useful and agreeable to others. The sick will love your piety if it causes them to be charitably consoled. Your family will love it if it makes you more solicitous of their good, milder in the face of life's vicissitudes, and withal more amiable. Your spouse will love it to the extent to which your devotion makes you warmer and more affectionate. If your parents and friends see in you a greater frankness, helpfulness, and readiness to bend to their wills in those things that are not contrary to the will of God, they too will find your life of devotion attractive. And this, as much as possible, should be your aim.

50

The Imagination in Prayer

It is not possible to pray without employing the imagination and the understanding. Yet it cannot be doubted that we should make use of them only for the sake of moving the will, and then no more. Some say that it is not necessary to use the imagination to represent to ourselves the sacred humanity of the Savior. Not, perhaps, for those who are already far advanced on the mountain of perfection. But for those of us who are still in the valleys—though we wish to be climbing—I think it is expedient to make use of all our faculties, including the imagination.

This imagination, however, ought to be quite simple, serving as a sort of needle with which to thread affections and resolutions into our mind. This is the great road, from which we should not take leave until the light of day is a little brighter and we can see the little paths. It is true that these imaginings should not be tangled up in too many particularities, but should be simple. Let us remain a while longer in the low valleys.

51

The Peace of God

Strive to remain in that peace and tranquillity that our Lord has given you. "The peace of God," says St. Paul, "which passes all understanding, will keep your hearts and your minds in Christ Jesus" (Phil. 4:7). Do you not see that he says the peace of God "passes all understanding"? That is to teach you that you should never trouble yourself to have any sentiment other than that of the peace of God. Now, the peace of God is the peace that proves the resolutions we have taken for God and the path that God has ordained for us. Walk firmly in the way in which the providence of God has placed you, without looking either to the right or to the left. That is the way of perfection for you. This satisfaction of spirit—even if it be without savor—is worth more than a thousand delightful consolations. If God intends you to face some difficulties, you must receive them from his hand—the hand you have taken hold of—and you must not let go of him until he has brought you to the point of your perfection. You will see that God's providence will accomplish all things according to your intentions, provided they be entirely in conformity with his. What is needed of you is a courage that is a little more vigorous and resolute.

52

A Time of Illness

It is during this time of affliction that you ought to demonstrate to our Lord the love that you have so often promised him. Recommend yourself to the prayers of St. Louis, who, after having succored his sick soldiers, counted himself blessed to be dying too and uttered this prayer as his last words: "I will enter your house, O my God. I bow down toward your holy temple and give thanks to your name" (cf. Ps. 5:7; 138:2). Place yourself under the divine will, which leads you to what is best for you. Pray to our Lord that he will be your consolation, that he will allow you to understand that it is "through many tribulations" that you will "enter the kingdom of God" (Acts 14:22). These crosses and trials should be more precious to us than contentment and spiritual delight, because our Lord chose them for himself and chooses them for all his true servants (cf. Heb. 12:2).

53

❦

The Presence of God

To remain in the presence of God and to place oneself in the presence of God are two different things. To place ourselves in his presence, we must withdraw our souls from all other objects and make ourselves attentive to his presence. After we have placed ourselves in his presence, we can keep ourselves there by the action of our will or intellect: by either looking upon God, or looking upon something else for the love of him, or not looking at anything but instead speaking to him, or neither looking at him nor speaking to him but simply remaining where he has placed us, like a statue in its niche. And when, to this simple act of remaining there is joined some sentiment that we belong to God and that he is our all, then we ought to give earnest thanks for his goodness.

If a statue in a niche in the middle of a room were able to speak, and we were to ask it, "Why are you there?," it would reply, "Because my master the sculptor placed me here."

"But why do you not move?"

"Because he wishes me to remain immobile."

"But what use do you serve there? What does it profit you to remain there in this way?"

"It is not to serve myself that I exist, but to serve and to obey the will of my master."

"But him you cannot see."

"No," says the statue, "but he sees me and takes pleasure that I am where he has placed me."

"But would you not like to be able to move so that you could be nearer to him?"

"No, not unless he so commands me."

"Is there then nothing at all that you desire?"

"No, for I am where my master has placed me, and his good pleasure is the sole delight of my being."

How good a prayer this is, and how good it is to keep oneself in the presence of God in this way, by holding fast to his will and his good pleasure! Mary Magdalene was a statue in her niche when, without speaking a word or moving, and perhaps without even looking at him, she "sat at the Lord's feet and listened to his teaching" (Luke 10:39). When he spoke, she listened. When he stopped speaking, she stopped listening, and yet she remained there. A little child resting on his mother's bosom while the two of them sleep is truly in his good and most desirable place, even though she says not a word to him, nor he to her.

How happy we are when we want to love our Lord! Let us then love him, and let us not stop to reckon how little we do for his love, provided that we know that we will never wish to do anything except for his love. Can we not even say that we remain in the presence of God while we sleep? For we sleep in his sight, at his pleasure, and by his will, and he places us upon our beds like statues in their niches, and when we awaken, we find that he is there, near to us, that he has not budged and neither have we. We are in his presence; it is only our eyes that are shut.

54

❧

A Time of Separation

In truth, it is not clear that your affliction ought to have so violently oppressed your heart. Lift your eyes to heaven and see that this life is only the journey toward the one that we will live there. Four or five months of absence will soon pass by. If our habits and our senses — so prone to attend to the world and to this life — are overly sensitive when we are opposed or oppressed, we should correct this fault by the clarity of faith, which tells us that those who are about to finish their voyage well are happy. Blessed are they who know that they have never lost anything that God has received in his grace.

55

The Death of a Loved One

I have just learned of your great loss, which besets you with all of the sorrow that normally attacks those who are left behind in such a separation. It would not be right to say to you, "Do not cry." No, for it is only just and reasonable that you should cry a little in witness of your sincere affection, and in imitation of our dear Master, who wept over his friend Lazarus. You should not, however, cry at length, as do those who set all of their thoughts upon this miserable life and forget that we too are going to eternity, where, if we have lived well in this world, we will be reunited with our dear departed forever. It is hardly possible to prevent our poor hearts from feeling the weight of this life and the loss of those who were our delightful companions in it, but we must not for that betray the solemn profession that we have made to join our will inseparably to the will of our God. Let us adore this divine providence and say:

"Yes, we bless you, because everything that pleases you is good." With how much mildness ought we to receive in our hearts losses such as this one, since our hearts ought to have greater affection for heaven than for the earth. Let us pray to God for this soul and for the consolation of the bereaved.

56

Interior Desolation

Consider the great desolation that the Master suffered in the Garden of Olives. This beloved Son had asked his good Father for consolation and knew that it was not his will to grant it. Therefore, he thought of it no longer and was neither anxious nor worried. Instead he valiantly and courageously carried out the work of our redemption. You should do as he did. If the Father denies you consolations, think no more of the matter, and stiffen your courage for the work of your salvation on the Cross as if you were never again to descend from it, as if you were never again to find life peaceful and serene.

What is it that you desire? We must see and speak to God amid the thunder and lightning (Exod. 19:16). We must see him amid the bush and the fire and the thorns, and in order to do this, the truth is that we must put off the shoes from our feet (Exod. 3:5) and make a great sacrifice of our desires and affections. Yet the divine Goodness would not have called you to the path on which you are traveling without strengthening you for all this; it is for him to bring this work to completion (Phil. 1:6). Even if he takes long to accomplish it, be patient: the task requires it. In brief, for the honor of God, submit completely to his will, and do not believe that you can serve him better otherwise. For we never serve him well except when we serve him as he wishes.

Now, it is his will that you should serve him without delight or pleasure, and instead with repugnance and a troubled spirit. This service does not give you any satisfaction, but it contents him. It is not to your liking, but it is to his. Imagine that you were never to be delivered from your suffering: what would you do? You would say to God: "I am yours" (cf. Ps. 119:94). If my sufferings are agreeable to you, let them grow in number and duration. Do the same thing now. Accustom yourself to your work as if it were to last forever. You will find that when you cease to think of your deliverance, God will.

57

❦

Last Things

As to meditating upon death, judgment, and hell: this is a most useful practice. But such meditations ought always to end with hope and confidence in God, and not with fear and trembling. For they are dangerous when they end in fear, especially in the fear of death and hell.

It is necessary, therefore, that having represented to yourself the greatness of the pains and their eternity, and having excited within yourself the fear of them and made a resolution to serve God better, you must then represent to yourself the Savior on the Cross and run to him with arms outstretched. Then embrace his feet with interior acclamations full of hope: "O door of my hopes, your blood will be my safeguard!" "I am yours, Lord, and you will save me." Come to a rest in this affection, thanking our Savior for his blood, offering him to his Father for your deliverance, and praying that the Father will grant it. Do not fail to end the meditation with hope; otherwise you will derive no profit from it. And keep this rule perpetually. You should never finish your prayers except with confidence, which is the virtue most necessary for praying to God and the one that honors him the most.

58

❦

Prepare for Death

You have had a long and honorable life, always faithful to the holy Catholic Church, but you have also been much given to the world and the management of its affairs. It is a strange thing, but both experience and the experts attest that a horse, however brave and strong it may be, is easily misled by the scent of the wolf. You have been living in the world; it is not possible — even though you have only touched it with your feet — that you should not have been covered in its dust. Our fathers of old, Abraham and the others, customarily welcomed their guests by washing their feet; should we not wash the affections of our souls prior to receiving the hospitality of our good God in his paradise?

It is a matter of great reproach for a mortal to die without having prepared for death, but it is twice as serious for those to whom our Lord has given the gift of old age. Those who arm themselves before the warning bell has tolled are always better off than those who, when the commotion breaks out, are running here and there looking for helmet and shield. We should say our goodbyes to the world when we have the leisure to do so and retire bit by bit from our attachment to creatures.

Trees that the wind blows down are not fit to be transplanted because they have left their roots in the soil; whoever would move them to another place must carefully disengage their roots from the soil in order to do so. And inasmuch as we are to be transplanted from this miserable soil into the land of the living, we must pull back and disengage our affections from the world one after another. Those who depart unexpectedly are excusable for not having taken leave of their friends and for leaving in disarray, but not those who knew the hour of their departure ahead of time. We must be ready, and not in order to leave before the hour, but to await it tranquilly.

59

☙

Dying

You must await the end result of this illness with as much meekness as you can muster, with the perfect resolution to conform yourself to the divine will with respect to this loss, if an absence for a little while ought to be called a loss by those who, with God's help, will be restored by an eternal presence. Blessed is the heart that loves and cherishes the divine will in everything.

If only our hearts were to be fixed upon this holy and blessed eternity, we would then say to our friends: "Go, dear friends, go to that eternal Being in the hour he designates; we will follow right behind you. And since this time here below is given to us for the sake of eternity, and this world is populated in order to populate heaven, our going there will have accomplished all that we had to do." It is in this way that our ancestors admired the sacrifice of Abraham. What a father's heart!

Dying

Let us leave our children to the mercy of God, who left his own Son to our mercy. Let us offer to him the lives of our children, for he has given the life of his for us. In sum, we must keep our eyes fixed on heavenly providence, to which we ought to submit with humble hearts. May God bless you, and mark your heart with the eternal sign of his pure love. We must become holy in a very small way, and pour out everywhere we go the good and sweet odor of our charity. May God purify us with his holy love, and may we count all things as loss compared with it. May our Lord be the repose of our hearts and our bodies. Remain in peace in the gentle arms of divine providence and under the protecting mantle of our Lady.

60

※

The Passage of Time

Do they not pass by, these temporal years? The months dwindle to weeks, the weeks to days, the days to hours, and the hours to moments, and these are all that we possess, but we possess them only as they perish and make our days perishable. Yet this should only make those moments the more beloved. For this life is full of suffering, and our most solid consolation is that these moments pass and at length give way before that holy eternity which is prepared for us in abundance by the mercy of God, and for which our soul aspires unceasingly. Truly, I never think of eternity without my thoughts having a sort of sweetness. And if my soul did not have some sort of proportion to this infinity, how could I understand my own thoughts about it? It must be the case that a faculty capable of attaining an object must have some sort of likeness to it. When I sense my desire running after my thoughts about this same eternity, my peace grows without bounds, for I know that we desire with a true desire only those things that are possible. My desire, then, assures me that I can have eternity: what remains for me but to hope for it? And this hope is given to me by the knowledge of the infinite goodness of him who would not have created a soul capable of straining for eternity without giving him the means to attain it.

Thus we find ourselves at the foot of the crucifix, which is the ladder by which we pass from these temporal years to eternal ones. May this next year be followed by others, and may all of them be usefully employed for the conquest of eternity. Live a long, holy, and happy life among your own here below during these perishable moments, so that you may live again eternally in that unchanging happiness for which you yearn.

An Invitation

Reader, the book that you hold in your hands was published by Sophia Institute Press. Sophia Institute seeks to nurture the spiritual, moral, and cultural life of souls and to spread the Gospel of Christ in conformity with the authentic teachings of the Roman Catholic Church.

Our press fulfills this mission by offering translations, reprints, and new publications that afford readers a rich source of the enduring wisdom of mankind.

We also operate two popular online Catholic resources: CrisisMagazine.com and CatholicExchange.com.

Crisis Magazine provides insightful cultural analysis that arms readers with the arguments necessary for navigating the ideological and theological minefields of the day. *Catholic Exchange* provides world news from a Catholic perspective as well as daily devotionals and articles that will help you to grow in holiness and live a life consistent with the teachings of the Church.

In 2013, Sophia Institute launched Sophia Institute for Teachers to renew and rebuild Catholic culture through service to Catholic education. With the goal of nurturing the spiritual, moral, and cultural life of souls, and an abiding respect for the role and work of teachers, we strive to provide materials and programs that are at once enlightening to the mind and ennobling to the heart; faithful and complete, as well as useful and practical.

www.SophiaInstitute.com
www.CatholicExchange.com
www.CrisisMagazine.com
www.SophiaInstituteforTeachers.org